PRODUCT CREATION FORMULA

ULTIMATE GUIDE TO CREATING DIGITAL PRODUCTS

Product Creation Formula

Table of Contents

Introduction 5

Pick A Problem You Can Solve.. 6

Do Market Research Before Writing A Word 8

Pick A Title That Will Sell...10

Choose The Best Format To Create Your Product 12

Plan Your Entire Product With An Outline...15

Create It Yourself Or Outsource It 17

Write Your Sales Letter And Set Up Your Funnel 19

Conclusion 21

NOTICE
You Do NOT Have the
Right to Resell this Ebook!

Disclaimer

This e-book has been written for information purposes only. Every effort has been made to make this ebook as complete and accurate as possible. However, there may be mistakes in typography or content. Also, this e-book provides information only up to the publishing date. Therefore, this ebook should be used as a guide - not as the ultimate source.

The purpose of this ebook is to educate. The author and the publisher do not warrant that the information contained in this e-book is fully complete and shall not be responsible for any errors or omissions. The author and publisher shall have neither liability nor responsibility to any person or entity with respect to any loss or damage caused or alleged to be caused directly or indirectly by this ebook.

Introduction

If you have been online for any length of time, you have likely heard that "the money is in the list" and that "you need to have your own product" to make the most money online. These are good pieces of advice to follow, but if you have never created your own product before, it may seem mission impossible to complete this task.

Fortunately, creating your own product does not have to be mission impossible. In fact, many people who are equally as talented and even as less talented as you are have created their own products and are reaping the benefits from them. I'm not just talking about profits either, but building your own brand/reputation, having affiliates promoting your product, and more.

This ebook will help you learn exactly how to create your own product so that you can begin to experience profit and success online. You will see that the process is not as difficult as you think. You will learn what topic to choose, how to do market research for it, choosing the best title for your product, and more. You will even learn how to outsource all or part of it so that you can focus only on the parts you wish to work on, if any. Everything that is needed to create a product will be explained in this book.

Pick A Problem You Can Solve

One of the keys to successful digital product creation is picking a problem you can solve. Too often, many new Internet marketers will choose to create a product they like, but that usually doesn't solve a problem that is currently in the marketplace. As a result, there is no real demand for that product. The common result in this case is that the person will go to a great deal of time and effort to create his/her product, but when no or few sales comes through, the person becomes disillusioned by the prospect of making a profitable living online, calls it "a scam," and often returns to their dreary job, figuring it's the only way to "make it in the world."

To have an in-demand product, you need to create a product that solves a problem. If this problem is widespread throughout the industry, and you develop an effective solution for it, people from all across the industry will want to get their hands on your item, setting you up for some nice profits. Thus, it is critical that you find a problem you can solve, then develop a solution for it, whether it's an ebook with information of an effective solution for the problem, a software program that can alleviate the problem, a membership site with information and resources that can solve the problem, etc.

You may be wondering, "how do I identify a problem I can solve?" Here, you will need to do some observation and some research. Some of the best ways is to go to your favorite search engine, type in the industry or topic you are interested in along with "+ forums." This should bring up a list of online forums that serve the people in that industry or who deal with that topic. You can go to these forums and read about the current topics and issues being dealt with in that industry. You may have to register at these forums first in order to access some sections of them, but this is not the case at all forums.

If an issue or problem continues to be brought up by several members of a forum, chances are that this is a problem you can build a product around in an effort to solve or alleviate it. This is a problem that is demanding a solution, and you have the opportunity to provide that solution and make good profits by doing it, plus build your reputation as a problem solver and solution creator.

You can also read about various topics and information in online newsletters, magazines, and ezines related to your industry to find potential problems that you can build a product around. Oftentimes, there are statistics in publications regarding common problems people in an industry are facing; if the statistics indicate a great deal of people are struggling with that same problem or issue, you have a potential product idea to build around.

Do Market Research Before Writing A Word

As was described a bit in the last chapter, it is important to do market research before you begin building your product, whether that's an ebook, a software program, a membership site, etc. Many new Internet marketers will just rush into creating a product or having a product created based on what THEY think will work or that seems like a good idea to them. Many times, what THEY think will be a good product idea turns out to be a dud and leads to few or no sales. You must always keep in mind what your target market, your future customer base, wants. This is what will lead to sales of your product. This is why market research beforehand is critical to creating an in-demand product that will sell well and bring in the notable profits you are expecting.

As mentioned in the last chapter, use your favorite search engine (i.e. Google, Bing, Yahoo, etc.) to find forums related to your industry and see what people in that industry identify as an issue or problem. If this issue or problem is mentioned by many of them, chances are that that is something you can build a product around.

Similarly, you can use the search engine to find notable publications – newsletters, ezines, magazines – that relate to your industry or topic and see what leading experts in the field say about various issues, topics, and problems the industry is facing today. There are often statistics and research cited that identify issues and problems facing the industry, issues and problems that you can build a product around.

If you are writing an ebook with information to be used to solve or alleviate the issue or problem, you can use any experience you have in dealing with the problem in your ebook. However, that alone may not be enough to create a quality, in-demand ebook that people will want to purchase to alleviate the issue or problem. Thus, research will likely be needed.

First, you can use the tip above to find newsletters, ezines, and publications that relate to the industry or topic to learn what industry experts are saying about any problems impacting the industry. As mentioned, there are often statistics and research that back up how much of an issue or problem this is. There can also be statistics and research on possible solutions that you can include in your ebook to add to its value.

Think about keywords or main ideas related to the problem or issue facing the industry you have chosen and input them into the search engine to see what other results come up related to people facing this issue, possible solutions, statistics regarding this issue and possible solutions, etc. You can even find direct statistics, research, and results by inputting a search phrase like "PROBLEM + statistics" or "PROBLEM + research," where PROBLEM equals the problem or issue facing the industry you have chosen.

Another way to expand your search in the search engines is to modify the types of results you get. You can scan for images, videos, .pdf documents, and more; this can often lead to different research reports that you may be able to use in your ebook or other product, and some of the specialized documents (especially .pdf documents) may not appear in a regular, unspecified search. Regarding images and videos, if you plan to use any of them in your product, be sure that they can be used for commercial use- modify the appropriate search engine result setting to ensure that all search results bring back results that can be used commercially.

Pick A Title That Will Sell

When creating a product, especially an ebook, you have to pick a title that will sell. Though the common saying "don't judge a book by its cover" is used often in contemporary language, unfortunately, most people WILL judge a book by its cover. This especially holds true for digital products because people can't get to hold a physical product in their hands; thus, they only have the cover and the title to go by. This is why your title must be one that will entice people to buy your product.

Thus, the title of your product must be interesting and must draw attention to it. One way of drawing attention to it is by indicating that it will solve the noted problem or issue in question. For instance, if the industry you have chosen, say, Internet marketing, is having an issue with getting qualified traffic to their websites, the title of your ebook could be, "Online Traffic Guide: Getting Qualified Traffic To Your Site."

The title needs to be descriptive enough to alert interested people as to what content is within its covers, yet it should not be so long that it turns off the readers and makes them think that the book isn't worth purchasing. As in the example above, a good title often will have a subtitle with it; this way, you can give a little more description on exactly what your product will offer in terms of content.

If you are having trouble coming up with a suitable title, look at other competing products in your industry, both those that attempt to address the problem or issue you have selected, if any, and other problems or issues within the industry. Look at their titles and see if there are any formats you can use to craft your title around. For instance, if another ebook on forum marketing is called, "Forum Marketing: How To Build Your Community of Loyal Followers," you could potentially call your traffic book from the previous example, "Website Traffic: How To Build A Constant Inflow of Traffic To Your Site."

Be sure to check Amazon.com (and even the country-specific Amazon sites, such as Amazon.co.uk) and see what books are popular and selling, especially those related to your industry and the specific problem you have identified. See what titles are selling well and modify your title accordingly, using those titles as a blueprint to craft your best title. Note, NEVER take a title word-for-word or even use most of the words so that your title looks like it was copied from another's product, but use a similar structure to craft your own title.

By looking at the popular-selling titles on Amazon and other online bookstores (Barnes & Noble, Google Books, Apple's iBooks via iTunes, etc.), you can learn what people are drawn to when it comes to titles (and graphics as well) and pattern your own book accordingly.

Choose The Best Format To Create Your Product

As was alluded to earlier in this book, you need to decide whether you are going to create an ebook, a software program, a membership site, an e-course (i.e. series of emails that dive into a topic or issue in depth), etc. You need to know your target market well enough to determine which format they prefer, as well as what format will be able to best deliver the information/solution so that the problem is solved or alleviated.

If you are creating an ebook, you need to determine whether you should create it in .txt (text format), .doc or .docx (Microsoft Word format), .rtf (Rich Text Format, which allows for more styling elements than .txt), .odt (OpenOffice/LibreOffice's format, similar to .doc and .docx formats), .pdf (Portable Document Format, capable of being opened by Adobe Reader and other similar PDF reader programs), .exe (executable file on Microsoft Windows machines), or another format. The format you choose will help to determine what elements you can include in your ebook.

In the earlier days of the Internet, (i.e. late-90s, early 2000s), many ebooks were in .exe format, as most Internet users were using Microsoft Windows computers and ebook generation wasn't as easy to accomplish as it is today. However, being that there are more Internet users using Mac computers and Linux-based computers, .exe format is rarely if ever used anymore because those Internet users would be left out unless they used some type of conversion program, with varying degrees of success in how the ebook was converted to their operating system.

Additionally, many Internet users read their ebooks on mobile operating systems, such as Apple's iOS, Google's Android operating system, and Amazon's modified Android operating system, among others. That is all the more reason why ebooks are rarely created in .exe format anymore; many are now created in .pdf, as most devices regardless of operating system can open a .pdf ebook, as Adobe Reader software is usually included on most devices, whether it would be a PC, laptop, or mobile device (smartphone, tablet, etc.). Most devices can also read .doc or

.docx files, as Microsoft has extended its Word program to iOS and even as a downloadable app. Thus, .doc or .docx is another good file format to consider when creating an ebook. Plus, most word processing programs, including Microsoft Word, OpenOffice, and LibreOffice, give you the ability to convert your .doc or .docx file into a .pdf file with just one click on the dashboard, making .doc to .pdf almost the preferred choice among most ebook creators today.

If you're creating a software program, it is preferable if the program can work on all operating systems, not just Windows, as there are many Mac users out there. Additionally, because many Internet users access files, services, and more via their mobile devices, it is preferable that these programs can work on a mobile device as well, as not everyone prefers or has easy access to a PC or laptop.

This is why many software developers are now using cloud-based technology to allow their users to access their software programs from anywhere via any device, whether it would be PC, laptop, smartphone, or tablet. Additionally, many Internet users like the idea of being able to use a software program from anywhere and not having to download it onto each machine on which they wish to use it. Many Internet users are not fond of the hassle of downloading software programs onto their machines or devices because of the amount of time and data usage they will have to use to download these programs.

Thus, if you plan on creating a software program to address the problem or issue you have identified, it would be wise to use cloud-based technology, including having a cloud-based server, so that people can access your program from anywhere on any device and not have to download anything to use it.

If you plan on creating a membership site, be sure to utilize a large-enough server so that you can continue to add content over time to the membership site, while also ensuring that people can access the site in a timely fashion. If you don't use a large-enough Web server with enough bandwidth, it may take forever for people to access it during heavy spikes in traffic, which will result in people getting frustrated and leaving your site to never return. If they are on a recurring subscription to use your site and its content, they will likely cancel if they can't access and use the site in a timely fashion. Also be sure that your membership site is mobile-friendly, as people may want to access it and use the content on their mobile devices while they are out and about and have a few minutes of free time. People will be turned out and willing to cancel their recurring subscriptions if they can't access and use your site if they are away from their PCs and/or laptops.

If you're creating an email series that dives into a problem and provides a remedy on how to solve it, be sure that people can access the email series either via their inboxes and/or via downloading it to their PCs, laptops, and/or mobile devices. Again, you must take into consideration how your product will look on mobile devices and ensure that your customers can use your product whether they choose to use it or you will run the risk of people not continuously using your product and not purchasing your future product offers.

Plan Your Entire Product With An Outline

Many new product creators will dive right into product creation, then run into issues as they go along because they decide to change something or because they forgot to add something and need to go back and add it, etc. This can cause unforeseen complications and make the process of product creation much more difficult than it needs to be.

A good way to avoid such difficulty is to create an outline of your entire product at the very beginning before you do any work (or have any work done) on it. Create an outline of exactly what your product will have in it, whether it's information in an ebook or email series, what features your software program will have, what sections your membership site will have, etc.

Take some time at the very beginning to determine exactly what information/features/sections your product will have. You know what will make it a valuable product that will solve or alleviate the problem your target market is having. Thus, you need to ensure that information/features/sections are in there, and you need to ensure it's in an easy-to-use or easy-to-digest manner so your target market will get the most benefit from it.

Making an outline of your product before you begin work on it will help to ensure you remain on track and put in the information/features/sections you wish to put into the product without adding extraneous information/features/sections that are not needed and that will be seen as "fluff" or a nuisance by your customers. Additionally, if you choose to outsource all or part of the product to others, having an outline will help to ensure you instruct your outsourcers on exactly what needs to be in their completed work to ensure your product is completed in a timely fashion and has everything in it that you are expecting to be in it.

If you are creating an ebook or email series, be sure to identify the problem that you are attempting to solve or alleviate, lay it out in a way to show the seriousness of the issue and why it has to be resolved or alleviated, then lay out your solution in a step-by-step manner to ensure that people can understand how and why it works and be able to implement it.

If you are creating a software program, be sure to lay out exactly how your software program alleviates or solves the problem you have identified, then show your customers/users how to use the software program to alleviate or solve that problem. It's often beneficial to post one or more videos and show them exactly how the software solves or alleviates the issue and exactly how to operate the software so that the software can solve or alleviate the issue.

If you are creating a membership site, be sure to lay out exactly what the membership site contains, how it alleviates or solves the problem, and the best way or sequence to use the site so that the user's problem is alleviated or solved. It often helps to have one or more videos within the site to show exactly what the different sections are and how they work in conjunction with each other to alleviate or solve the problem in question. Those videos should also show the best way or sequence to use the site in order to maximize the effectiveness of the site and the content within to solve or alleviate the problem in question.

Create It Yourself Or Outsource It

As alluded to in the last chapter, you have the choice of creating the entire product yourself or to outsource all or part of the product to one or more outsourcers. You need to consider the pros and cons of both approaches to decide if you want to create all of your product, create part of your product and let outsourcers create part of it, or if you want outsourcers to create all of it.

If you create all of the product yourself, you will have total control of it. You will know exactly what goes into it because you will be the one who puts it there. You know what you are wanting in the product, so you know it will go in there because you will be the one doing it. Thus, there is very little chance of some unexpected surprise occurring of missing information/features/sections because you will be in direct control of everything.

Unfortunately, this also means that you will need to take the necessary time to input all of that information/features/sections into the product. Thus, you will have to take time away from other projects, other areas of your business, etc., as you need to ensure that everything gets done in the manner you want it done to ensure that it is completed properly.

This is why many product creators and Internet marketers will utilize outsourcers for all or part of their product projects. Utilizing outsourcers in this manner will allow them to still have overall control of the process without having to do all or any of the work required, enabling them to work on other projects that need their direct intervention and/or work on other aspects of their business.

Unfortunately, working with outsourcers also has its cons or negatives. It can often be difficult to find capable, trustworthy outsourcers to give you exactly what you are looking for. They may have a specific idea in mind when you describe your project and it doesn't match up with what you have in mind. Additionally, you also have to ensure they continue to work in a timely fashion to ensure your project doesn't take forever to become a reality. Normally, these outsourcers are not located near your location, so it can often be difficult to communicate with them and stay updated on their progress and any issues they might have in completing the project.

In fact, in many cases, the outsourcers can be on the other side of the world; thus, time zone differences can play a major factor in communication between you and them. They may be asleep when you're awake, and vice-versa, etc. Thus, it can be difficult to stay in contact and ensure that the project is being done in the manner you want it done and in the timely fashion you want it completed in.

Thus, you need to weigh the pros and cons to doing the project entirely yourself, having outsourcers doing the project entirely, or you and them splitting the work. Consider the matter carefully before proceeding with your project.

If you choose to outsource all or part of the project, there are several outsourcing websites you can go to in order to find the person or persons with the requisite skills needed to complete your project. This can include researching and writing content for your ebook and/or email series, creating the ebook cover and banner ads for promoting your ebook, creating the software program you wish to have for your product, creating the software platform and site for your membership site, etc. Some of these websites include Fiverr, Elance, Guru, Upwork, SolutionInn, and PeoplePerHour- consult the accompanying Product Creation Blueprint Resource List for more information on these outsourcing websites.

If you have friends in the industry, you can also ask them to see who they would recommend to help you complete your product project. They may know some outsourcers who have done good work for them in the past and who are trustworthy, which can aid you in finding quality outsourcers quickly and ensuring your projects get completed in a timely and professional manner.

Write Your Sales Letter And Set Up Your Funnel

Once you have decided on what type of product you are going to create to alleviate or solve the problem you have decided upon and have determined how it is going to be created, you are ready to begin writing your sales letter and setting up your funnel. Both of these are critical to selling your product effectively; after all, people are not going to buy your product if they are not convinced of its ability to help them alleviate or solve the problem you have targeted.

If you are experiencing in copywriting, you can likely write your own sales letter that accentuates why your product can alleviate or solve the problem that the industry is facing. However, most people are not that proficient in copywriting, so many will either outsource this work as well or use some type of software program, sales letter template, and/or copywriting formula to help them create a sales letter.

All of these are viable options to creating your sales letter; you will need to choose what works best for you for your specific project. With all sales letters, you especially need to focus on the headline; if the headline is weak and doesn't identify why people should pay attention to your offer, they won't read the rest of it, and you will have lost the sale.

When it comes to your sales funnel, you need to determine the sequence based on what you have to offer. Most Internet marketers will offer more than just a "front-end" product (i.e. your main offer), as many sales and most profits will occur on the "back-end" of the funnel. This is what many in the Internet marketing industry call the "one-time offers" or "OTOs."

Most OTOs involve providing a more advanced version of the product, whether that's audios and videos that go with an ebook or email series, a more advanced software program with additional features and benefits, access to additional sections within a membership site that provides more benefits to the user, etc. Usually, these OTOs are higher-priced than the original offer; they can also be recurring monthly or annual payments.

The idea behind building your sales funnel is that research has shown that consumers are more willing to purchase a cross-sell or upsell offer at the same time they have purchased an item. A cross-sell example is when someone orders a burger at a fast food restaurant and then orders fries and a soft drink at the same time. An upsell example is when you buy a tool and then buy the accessories with it to make it a more powerful and/or useful tool. The same concepts apply to Internet marketing, which is why having a sales funnel is essential to maximizing your sales and profits.

Creating an Internet marketing sales funnel means that the prospect will purchase your main offer, then will be presented with an upgrade offer (i.e. OTO). If he/she purchases that offer, there could be another upgrade offer after that or it could lead to the download area, membership site, etc. If the person rejects the upgrade offer, it could lead to a less expensive and less feature-laden upgrade offer or it could lead to the download area, membership site, etc. You must plan out your sales funnel carefully based upon what offers you have to offer to your target market to alleviate or solve their problem so that you can maximize your sales and profits.

Conclusion

In this ebook, you have learned what it takes to create your own product and why you should create your own product. You have learned to identify a problem you can solve by looking at related industry forums, newsletters, publications, and more. You utilize the knowledge you have and market research you conduct via the search engines in order to create a solution to the problem you have identified.

You need to choose a title that draws people's attention and informs them of the problem you can solve or alleviate for them. You can look at the best-selling titles on sites like Amazon, Barnes & Noble, Google's Books section, and Apple's iTunes Bookstore to learn what title format work well to draw people's attention and use them as a template or format to give your book the best, most interesting title possible.

You need to determine whether your product will be an ebook, a software program, a membership site, an email series, some other format, or a combination of any or all of the above. You learned why creating an outline can help to ensure that you provide all of the necessary information/features/sections so that your product has the value you intended and solves or alleviates the problem you identified.

You learned the pros and cons of creating the product yourself versus using outsourcers to complete it. You learned that you can do all of the work yourself, have the outsourcers complete all of the work themselves, or you can split the work between you and themselves as you choose to divide it.

You learned the benefits of having a strong sales letter, including showing your target market the benefits of having your product to solve or alleviate their problem. You learned why you need to have a carefully-constructed sales funnel made up of one or more upgrade offers (also known as "one-time offers" or "OTOs") and what those upgrade offers can be. You learned that consumers will be more likely to purchase cross-sell or upsell offers after they have purchase the main offer, which is why you need your sales funnel in place when you present your offer.

By following the information in this book, you will be able to identify a problem you can solve in your chosen industry/niche, create your own digital product to solve that problem, create a sales letter and sales funnel for that product, and gain the benefits, reputation, and profits from having your own product.

Good luck!

PRODUCT CREATION FORMULA

ULTIMATE GUIDE TO CREATING DIGITAL PRODUCTS

Product Creation Formula Checklist

Pick a Problem You Can Solve

- ☐ Pick a problem that you can solve that is wanted by your target market, not what YOU think will work.
- ☐ An in-demand product is one that will solve a problem.

Do Market Research Before Writing A Word

- ☐ Use your favorite search engine to find forums related to your industry and see what people in that industry identify as a problem or issue.
- ☐ Look at related industry forums, newsletters, publications, other sources to learn what problems you can potentially solve.
- ☐ If you have experience dealing with the issue or problem in question, you can use that experience in your book as well to make your more product more unique and valuable.
- ☐ Be sure to find and use relevant research and statistics from noted industry publications and experts in your book.
- ☐ Use keywords or main ideas related to the problem or issue in the search engine to see what results come up you can also include in your book.
- ☐ Modify the types of results you get in the search engines (images, videos, .pdf documents, etc.) to find more data and research.

Pick A Title That Will Sell

- ☐ Your title must be interesting and must draw attention to it in order for it to sell well.
- ☐ Be sure the title notes the problem or issue it will solve to alert people to what the information inside will do.

- Make sure the title isn't so long that it sounds boring and turns people off from buying it.
- Many good titles have subtitles.
- Look at comparable books on the same or similar topics that sell well, see if you can model (NOT copy) your title after theirs.
- Check Amazon, Barnes & Noble, other online bookstore sites with titles that sell well, model (NOT copy) your title after theirs.

Choose The Best Format To Create Your Product

- Decide on whether you are creating an ebook, software program, membership site, email series, audio product, video product, etc.
- If creating an ebook, decide on such formats as .txt (text format), .doc or .docx (Microsoft Word format), .rtf (Rich Text Format, which allows for more styling elements than .txt), .odt (OpenOffice/LibreOffice's format, similar to .doc and .docx formats), .pdf (Portable Document Format, capable of being opened by Adobe Reader and other similar PDF reader programs), .exe (executable file on Microsoft Windows machines).
- .Pdf ebooks are the most popular now because they can be read on virtually any operating system and even on mobile devices.
- If you're creating a software product, creating it on a cloud-based platform will allow users to access and use the software from anywhere, even on a mobile device.
- If you're creating a membership site, be sure to use a large-enough server so that it can hold all present and future data, be sure it's mobile-friendly, and be sure to use a platform or plugin that ensures the right people get access to the site and denies all others who should haven't access.

Plan Your Entire Product With An Online

- Creating an outline of your entire product before you begin creating the product can help to avoid unforeseen complications and keep the process of product creation from being more difficult than it needs to be.

- An outline can help make any type of product (ebook, software program, membership site, email series, etc.) creation easier.
- Take some time at the very beginning to determine exactly what information/features/sections your product will have.
- Creating an outline at the beginning can help to ensure that the information/features/sections you want your product to have will be in there at the end.

Create It Yourself Or Outsource It

- Decide whether you yourself will create the product, you will use outsourcers to create all of it, or you and they will both create the product.
- If you create the entire product yourself, you will have total control over it and ensure everything you want is in there.
- However, if you create the entire product yourself, it will require your full attention, thus diverting your focus away from other projects and other aspects of your business.
- Utilizing outsourcers for your product creation will allow you to focus on other projects that need your direct involvement and on other aspects of your business.
- However, finding trustworthy, capable outsourcers can be difficult, and their ideas and ways of doing things may not exactly line up with what you have in mind; thus, challenges and revisions may arise as a result, which can also take time to resolve.
- Communication with outsourcers may be difficult due to their being in a different timezone, even being halfway around the world.
- Some notable outsourcer websites include Fiverr, Elance, Guru, Upwork, SolutionInn, and PeoplePerHour.
- Ask for recommendations.

Write Your Sales Letter And Set Up Your Funnel

- ☐ If you are experienced - write your own convincing sales letter.
    - Use a Template
    - Follow a copywriting formula
    - Focus on the headline
    - Use sub-headlines
    - Be sure to focus on the benefits; what is in it for him/her?

- ☐ If you are not experienced – Outsource It

Product Creation Formula Resource List

Search Engines (for research of your target market and competitors to help identify a problem you can solve):

Google- https://www.google.com

Bing- https://www.bing.com

Yahoo- https://www.yahoo.com

Outsourcing Websites (to outsource product creation work):

Fiverr- http://www.fiverr.com All types of jobs listed here start at $5, with Level 2 sellers capable of selling additional services for more. Services include editing, video making, writing, graphic design, and more.

Elance- http://www.elance.com Many freelancers here in many different categories- can communicate with them on-site. You can pay part of the total amount of a job for each milestone that is completed, unlike most freelancing sites.

Guru- http://www.guru.com Have freelancers in graphic design, programming, writing, and more. The site will suggest specific "gurus" based on your project requirements.

Upwork- http://www.updesk.com Formerly known as Odesk.com, over 500,000 businesses use them, making them one of the most popular freelancing websites. You can request and review screenshots of a freelancer's work while the project is worked on.

SolutionInn- http://www.solutioninn.com Similar to Fiverr's set-up in that experts set up services and set fixed prices.

PeoplePerHour- http://www.peopleperhour.com Similar to Fiverr and SolutionInn in that freelancers can set up their services and set fixed prices, but unlike Fiverr, also allows freelancers to search through listings and find jobs on their own. Has a vast array of services offered, including translation services, creating tutorials, programming, writing, graphic design, and more.

More Sites To Conduct Market Research:

Amazon- http://www.amazon.com

Barnes & Noble- https://www.barnesandnoble.com/

Apple's iBooks via iTunes- https://itunes.apple.com/us/app/id364709193 (only accessible via iTunes on PC/Mac/iOS).

Google Books- https://books.google.com/

Tools For Product Creation:

Microsoft Word (for text documents)- https://products.office.com/en-us/word

Microsoft Excel (for spreadsheets)- https://products.office.com/en-us/excel

Microsoft Powerpoint (for presentations and slides)- https://products.office.com/en-us/powerpoint

Microsoft Office (combinations of all of the aforementioned Microsoft tools)- https://products.office.com/products/

Apache OpenOffice (free alternative to Microsoft Office)- http://www.openoffice.org/

LibreOffice (another free alternative to Microsoft Office)- http://www.libreoffice.org/

Adobe Reader (Adobe's free PDF reader that enables Internet users to read PDF documents)- https://acrobat.adobe.com/us/en/acrobat/pdf-reader.html

FoxIt Reader (alternative to Adobe Reader)- https://www.foxitsoftware.com/downloads/

CutePDF Writer (alternative to Adobe Reader)-
http://www.cutepdf.com/Products/CutePDF/writer.asp

Other Useful Internet Marketing Resources:

GoDaddy- A domain registrar that allows you to research and purchase your domain name that is needed for your website:
https://www.godaddy.com

Namecheap- Another domain registrar that allows you to research and purchase your domain name that is needed for your website:
https://www.namecheap.com

HostGator- A prominent and experienced Web hosting provider that allows you to host your website online: https://www.hostgator.com

BlueHost- Another prominent and experienced Web hosting provider that allows you to host your website online: https://www.bluehost.com

WordPress- What many Internet marketers use to create their websites and blogs: https://wordpress.org/download/

www.ingramcontent.com/pod-product-compliance
Lightning Source LLC
Chambersburg PA
CBHW081709220526

45466CB00009B/2932